SPOT 50
Cats

Camilla de la Bedoyere

First published in 2011 by Miles Kelly Publishing Ltd
Harding's Barn, Bardfield End Green, Thaxted, Essex, CM6 3PX, UK

This edition printed in 2012

2 4 6 8 10 9 7 5 3 1

Publishing Director Belinda Gallagher
Creative Director Jo Cowan
Editors Amanda Askew, Sarah Parkin
Designer Kayleigh Allen
Production Manager Elizabeth Collins
Reprographics Stephan Davis, Jennifer Hunt

ISBN 978-1-84810-598-0

Printed in China

British Library Cataloguing-in-Publication Data
A catalogue record for this book is available from the British Library

ACKNOWLEDGEMENTS
The publishers would like to thank the artist Ian Jackson who has contributed to this book

All other images are from the Miles Kelly Archives

Made with paper from a sustainable forest

www.mileskelly.net
info@mileskelly.net

www.factsforprojects.com

CONTENTS

Tick the circles when you have spotted the species.

TYPES OF CAT

Cats have lived with people for thousands of years. During that time they have been bred to develop certain characteristics of appearance and personality. Breeds, or types, have been developed, such as Siamese or Asian Self, and are still being developed today.

PEDIGREE CATS

These are the 'top quality' animals of a certain breed. They can be expensive to buy and sometimes have particular health problems. However, they have been bred for their beauty and appealing characters, so pedigrees are a popular choice for cat-lovers.

NON-PEDIGREE CATS

Cats that have parents of mixed breeds are non-pedigree. They often have a mixture of characteristics that can give you a clue about the breeds they are descended from. Non-pedigree cats tend to live for a long time, up to 20 years or more.

LONGHAIR, SHORTHAIR OR FANCY?

Most cats have coats with long hair, semi-longhair or shorthair. In this book, long-haired and semi-longhaired cats are grouped together. Wire-haired and bald cats can be found in the Fancy section.

Persian Blue Longhair

Bombay

Peterbald

BODY AND COAT

Cats are usually described in terms of body shape and size, the type and colour of their fur, and the colour of their eyes. The shapes of their heads, ears and eyes are also used to distinguish between breeds.

Body could be slender and elegant, or stocky and powerful

Ears might be pointed or round, set wide or close

Eyes may be round, or almond-shaped

Tail may be long, short, fluffy or slender

Face may be wide, or long and thin

Paws may be round or oval, delicate or large

SIZE TO THE SHOULDER

Large: 40 cm, Medium: 25 cm, Small: 20 cm

COLOURFUL COATS AND MARKINGS

Tabbies are striped, Tortoiseshells have patches of red, black and white fur, and Blue cats are smoky blue-grey in colour. Some cats have a thick undercoat that is a different colour to the top-coat. Others have two or more colours appearing on a single strand of hair – this is described as 'flecked' or 'ticked'.

Blue

Tabby

Tortoiseshell

ASIAN SELF

These beautiful cats have large, expressive eyes and they like a lot of attention. They are active, energetic animals that love to play. Asian Selfs can become very attached to their owners, following them around and miaowing until they are stroked or entertained. Asian Selfs are very intelligent and good at solving problems, such as opening doors. They are healthy cats that can live for 15 years or more.

SMALL-MEDIUM

Asian Selfs have been used to breed other varieties, such as Bombays and Burmillas.

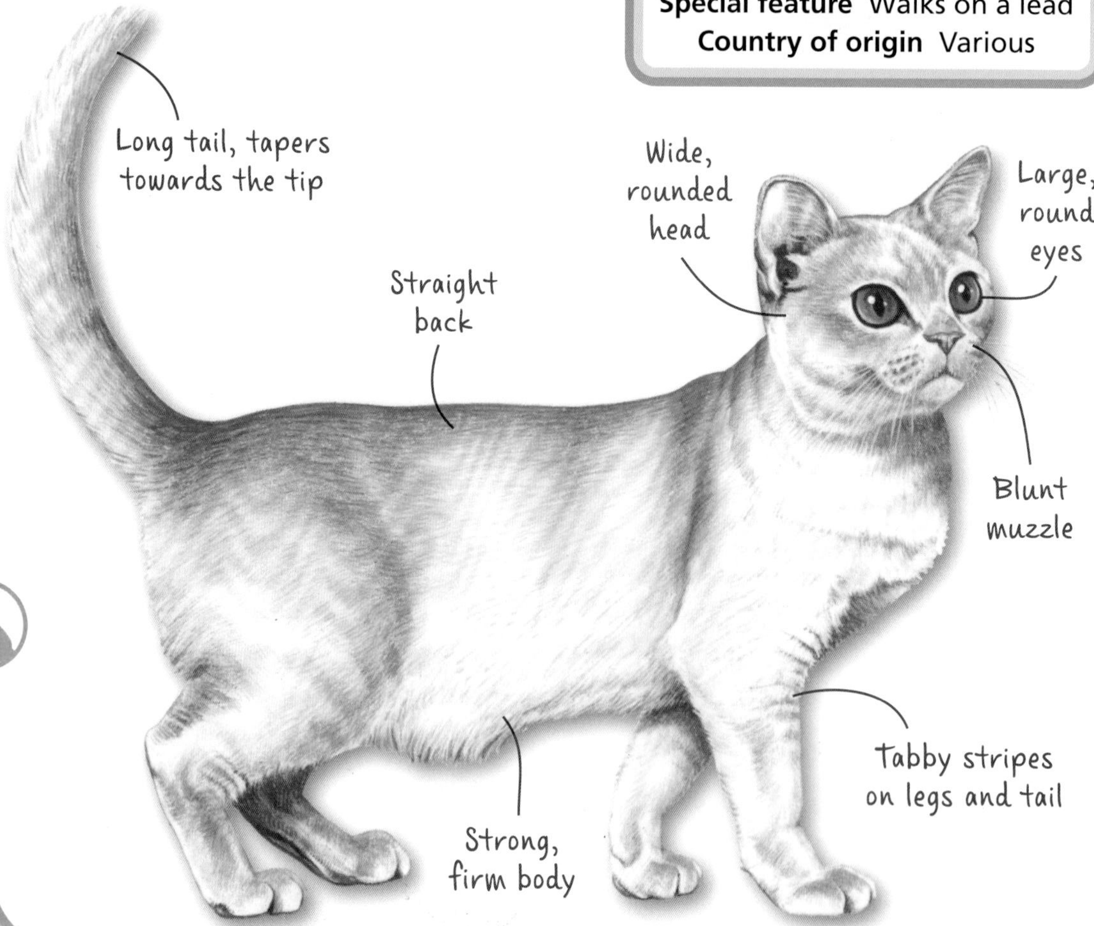

FACT FILE

Eye colour Yellow, gold or green
Fur colour Various including black, chocolate-brown, smokey-blue, reddish, and cream
Character Charming and energetic
Special feature Walks on a lead
Country of origin Various

Long tail, tapers towards the tip

Straight back

Wide, rounded head

Large, round eyes

Blunt muzzle

Strong, firm body

Tabby stripes on legs and tail

BENGAL

Although independent, Bengals like company. They were bred from a wild Asian cat and a Tabby, so they combine the qualities of both types. They have an athletic body and like to hunt, or take long trips to explore outdoors. Snow Bengals have light-coloured coats with dark markings. Their eyes are blue or blue-green.

MEDIUM-LARGE

Like their wild cat cousins, Bengals love to leap and they usually prefer to sit in high places so they can watch what is going on.

FACT FILE

Eye colour Gold, green, hazel or blue
Fur colour Spots and marbling on cream, orangey or brown fur
Character Independent and playful
Special feature Likes water
Country of origin USA

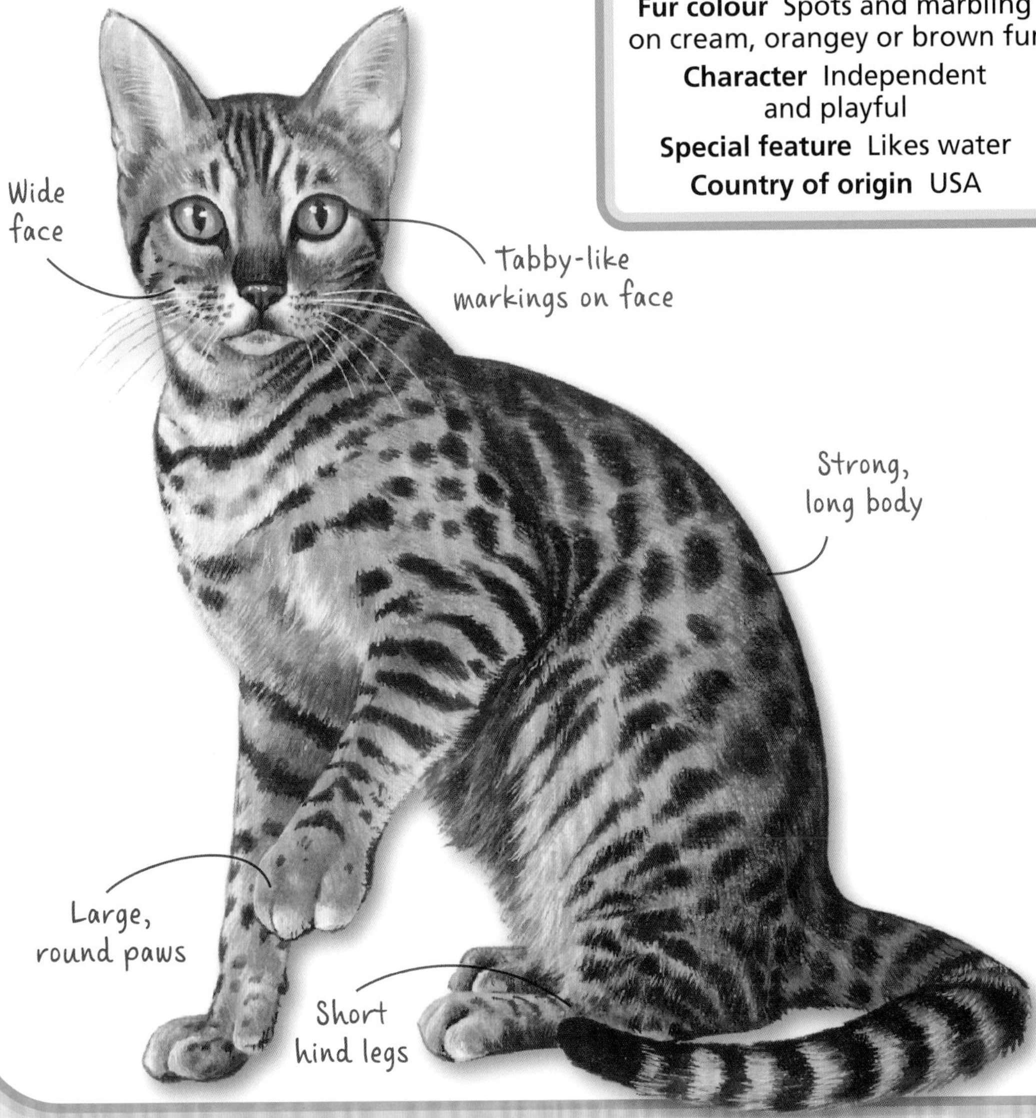

Wide face

Tabby-like markings on face

Strong, long body

Large, round paws

Short hind legs

BOMBAY

Originally bred from Burmese cats, **Bombays are black Asian Self cats.** These sociable animals love company and purr loudly when they are around people. Bombays have a lot of energy – they like to play and often sharpen their claws on furniture. They can be bossy, causing them to not get on well with other cats. However, Bombays have been known to bond with dogs.

SMALL–MEDIUM

This breed was developed in the 1950s by a breeder who wanted a domestic cat that looked like a small panther.

FACT FILE

Eye colour Gold, copper or yellow-green

Fur colour Black

Character Sociable and elegant

Special feature Shiny coat

Country of origin USA

Round, wide head

Large, round eyes

Long, sleek body

Dense but soft, glossy fur

Small paws with black pads

Long tail with a rounded tip

BRITISH BI-COLOUR SHORTHAIR

These cats can be recognized by their **coat of two colours that form solid patches of fur.** Black-and-white Bi-Colours are popular and are sometimes called Magpie cats. Cream-and-white Bi-Colours are more unusual. These cats make good family pets because they have lively, friendly personalities. Bi-Colours are curious, playful and intelligent. They are long-lived cats and can reach the age of 14 or more.

MEDIUM-LARGE

A Bi-Colour Shorthair once joined its owner who was imprisoned in the Tower of London. Legend says the cat climbed down the chimney!

FACT FILE

Eye colour Gold, orange or copper-orange
Fur colour Cream and white, red and white, blue and white, or black and white
Character Friendly and smart
Special feature Patched coat
Country of origin Various

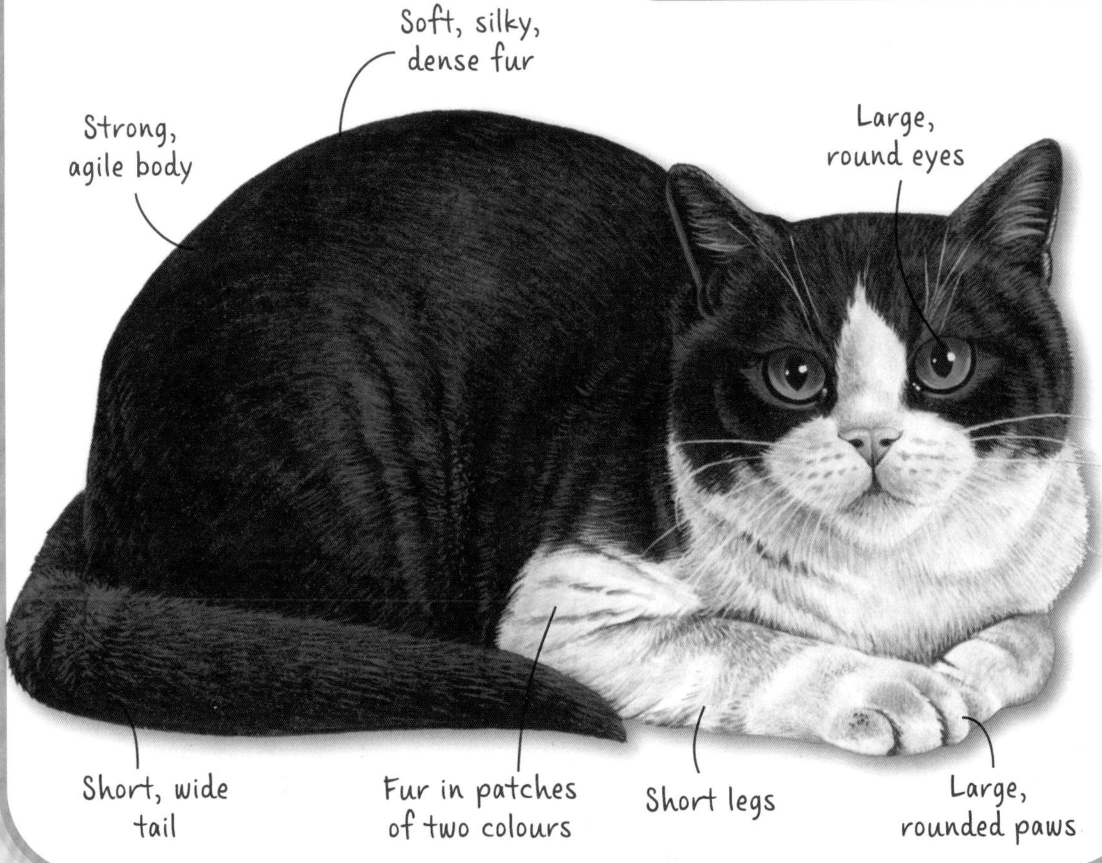

Soft, silky, dense fur

Strong, agile body

Large, round eyes

Short, wide tail

Fur in patches of two colours

Short legs

Large, rounded paws

BRITISH BLACK SHORTHAIR

One of the largest breeds of pet cat, **Black Shorthairs have tough, stocky bodies.** They are perfectly suited to hunting and a life outdoors. With a friendly nature, they enjoy the comfort of a warm home, but they also like to explore outside.

LARGE

These cats are skilled hunters. They prey on birds, and occasionally present their owners with dead mice.

FACT FILE

Eye colour Gold, orange or copper
Fur colour Black fur, with no white
Character Independent and intelligent
Special feature Good at hunting
Country of origin Various

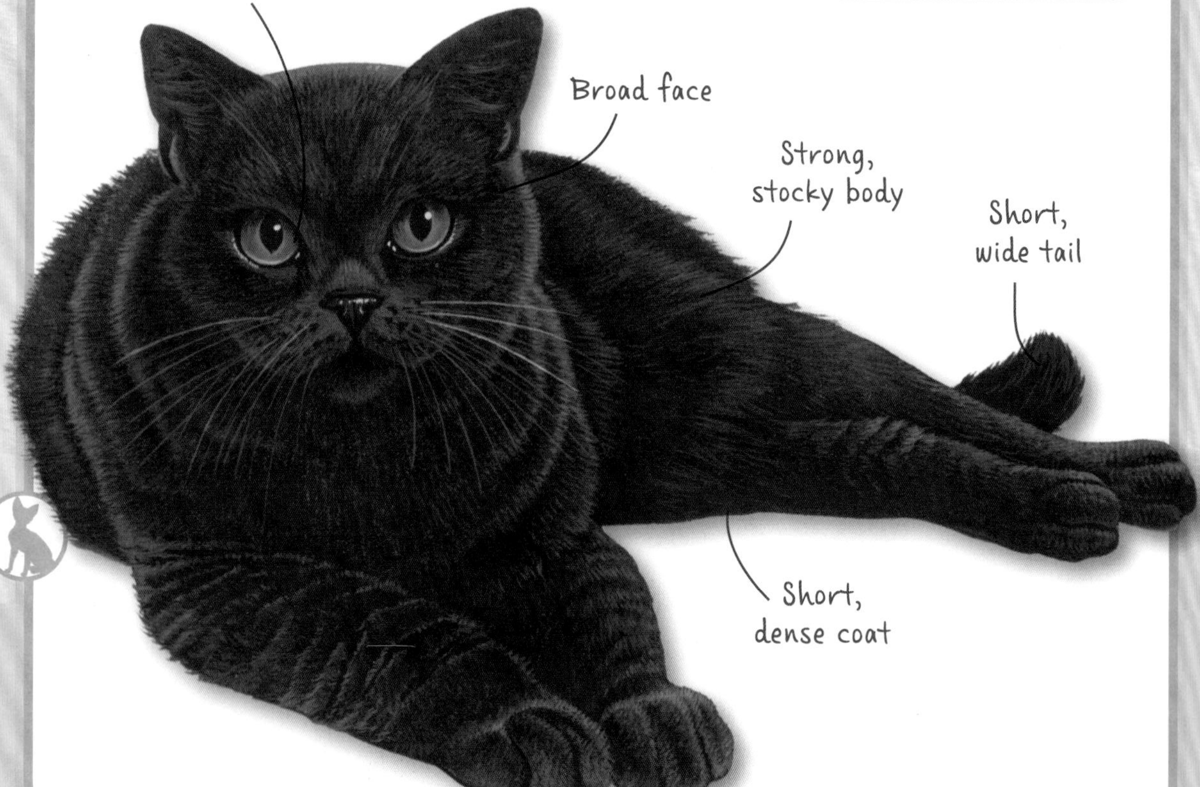

Large, attractive eyes (non-pedigree cats have green eyes)

Broad face

Strong, stocky body

Short, wide tail

Short, dense coat

BRITISH BLUE SHORTHAIR

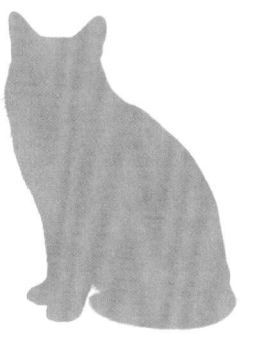

These fluffy cats may be described as shorthaired, but their coats are as dense and soft as the coats of many longhaired cats. Despite having strong, muscled bodies, Blue Shorthairs are not very energetic. They enjoy exercise, but are very happy to stay indoors and settle somewhere warm. These cats enjoy company.

MEDIUM-LARGE

Blue Shorthairs nearly died out more than 50 years ago. Their numbers grew again by breeding them with Blue Longhairs.

FACT FILE

Eye colour Gold
Fur colour Blue-grey
Character Loving and easy-going
Special feature Very soft fur
Country of origin Various

Round eyes

Large cheek pads give the cat a 'smiley' face

Snub nose with a blue nose pad

Stocky, muscular body

Short legs

Round paws with blue pads

BRITISH CREAM SHORTHAIR

Cream Shorthairs are quite rare because it is very difficult to breed them with the perfect colour. Ideally, they should be a solid cream colour all over, but most kittens are born with tabby stripes. As they age, the stripes may fade but most Cream Shorthairs still have some markings. They are good-natured and relaxed.

MEDIUM-LARGE

The tabby markings of a Cream Shorthair may fade with time, but hot and cold weather can make them reappear.

FACT FILE

Eye colour Gold or orange

Fur colour Cream base fur, usually with marmalade tabby markings

Character Calm and bright

Special feature Rare

Country of origin Various

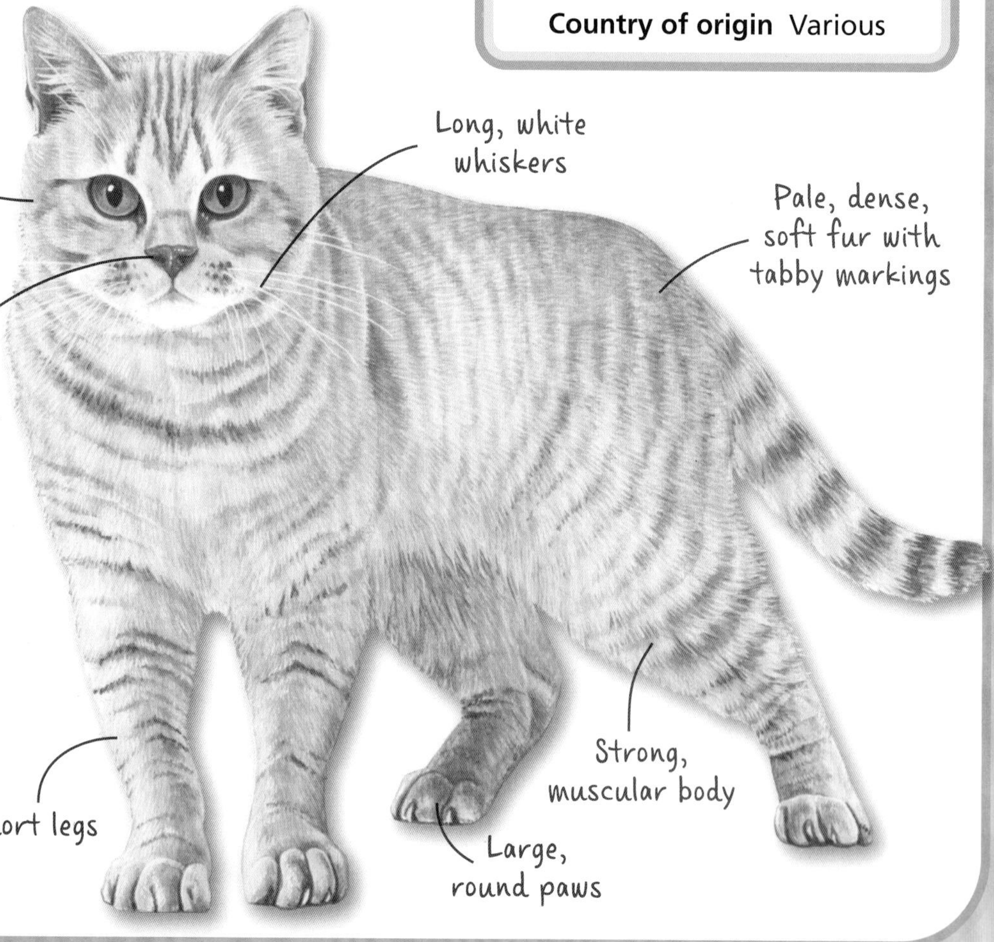

Wide face

Long, white whiskers

Pale, dense, soft fur with tabby markings

Pink nose pad

Short legs

Large, round paws

Strong, muscular body

BRITISH TORTOISESHELL SHORTHAIR

Almost all Tortoiseshell Shorthairs are female. Their unusual markings are linked to being female, so few males are born – those that are born are unlikely to be able to father kittens. They can vary in appearance and personality. They are affectionate, intelligent and good-natured.

MEDIUM-LARGE

Females may not produce any Tortoiseshell kittens in a litter, which means that the breed is still quite rare.

FACT FILE

Eye colour Orange or copper

Fur colour Patches of red, black and white, or cream

Character Clever and friendly

Special feature Unusual colours

Country of origin Various

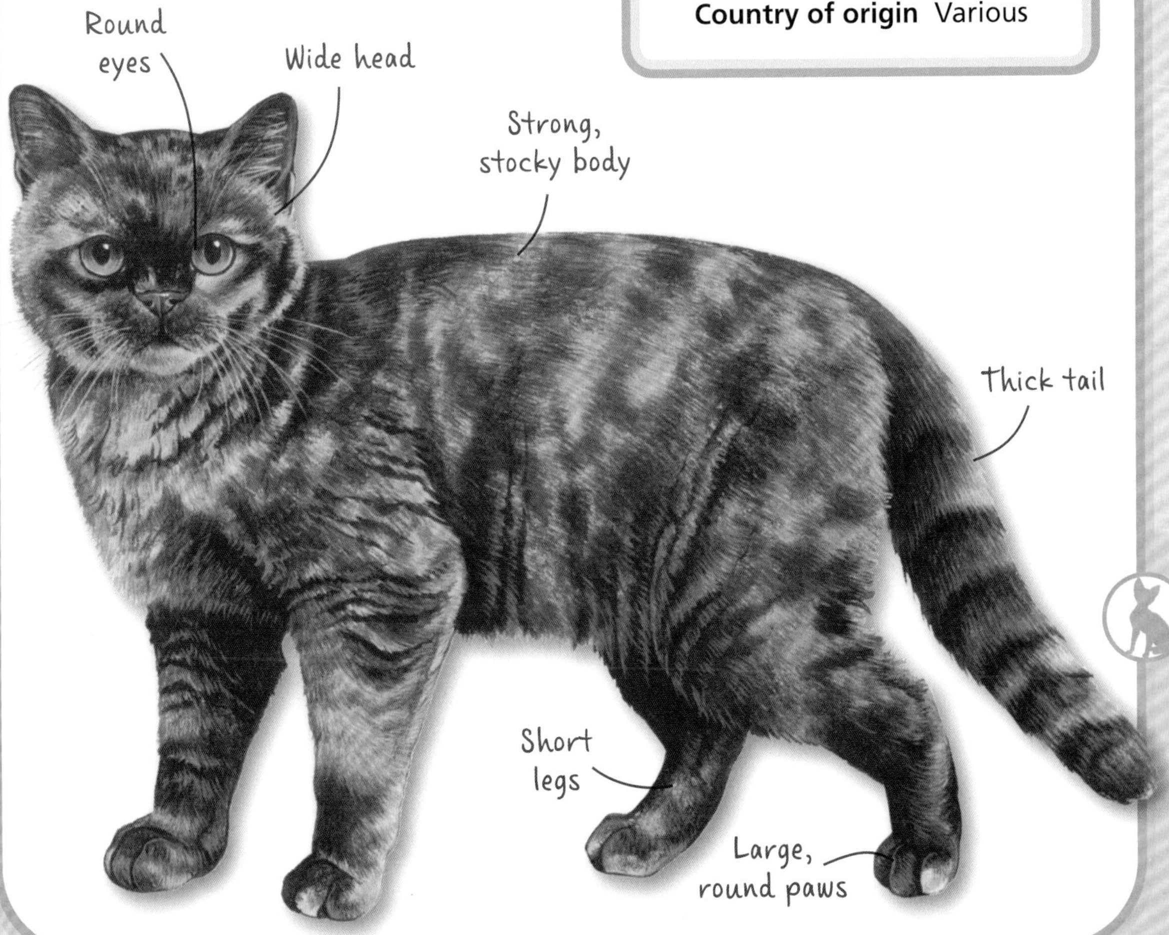

Round eyes

Wide head

Strong, stocky body

Thick tail

Short legs

Large, round paws

BRITISH WHITE SHORTHAIR

With a pure white coat, White Shorthairs occasionally have different-coloured eyes – one blue and one orange. They are heavy, well-built cats with short legs and tails. Blue-eyed cats often have hearing problems. White Shorthairs are gentle, friendly cats that are happy to be around children and like a quiet life indoors. These cats enjoy their food, and can become overweight if fed too much.

MEDIUM-LARGE

White Shorthairs with one blue eye and one orange eye are sometimes deaf in the ear closest to the blue eye.

FACT FILE

Eye colour Orange, blue or green

Fur colour White

Character Charming and friendly

Special feature Odd-coloured eyes

Country of origin Various

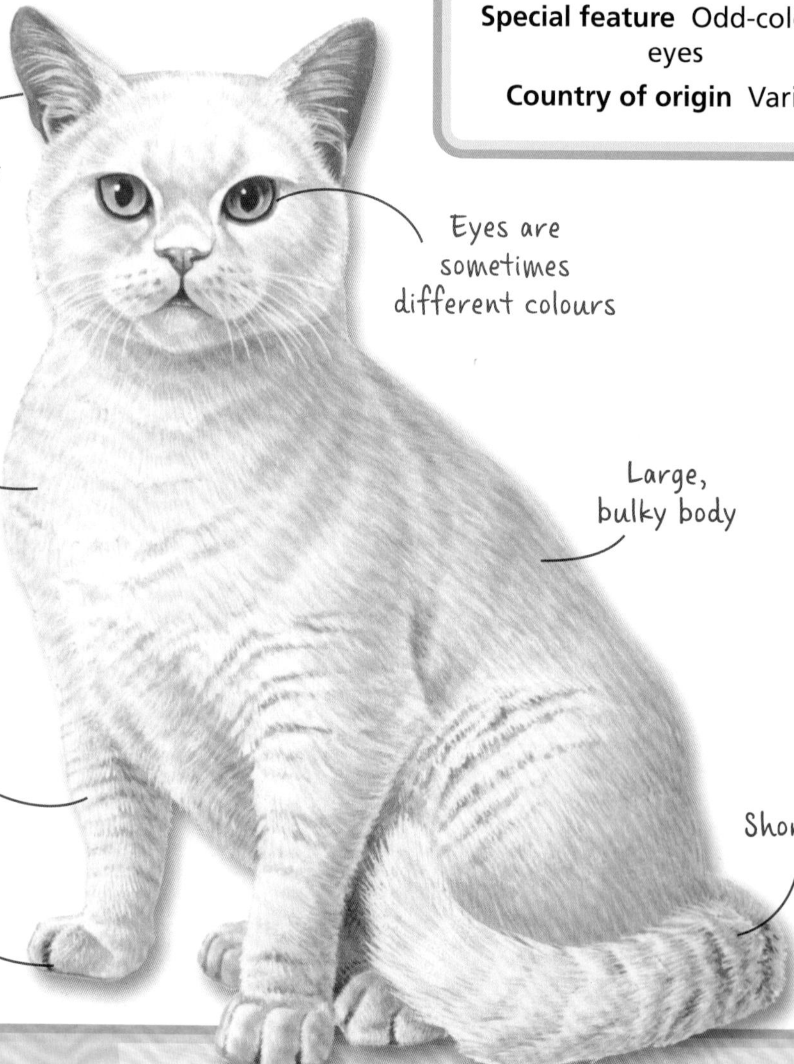

Ears are set well apart

Eyes are sometimes different colours

Thick fur

Large, bulky body

Short legs

Large, round paws

Short tail

BURMESE

Full of character, Burmese like to be the centre of attention and enjoy being with people. Burmese can get lonely if they have to spend whole days without company. They are very clever, and can be trained to fetch small things. Burmese tend to be very healthy and can live for up to 20 years.

SMALL—MEDIUM

Burmese were originally brown. Then a blue kitten was born, so breeders began to develop different colours.

FACT FILE

Eye colour Yellow or gold

Fur colour Various solid colours including black, brown, blue, red and cream

Character Tough and sociable

Special feature Long-lived

Country of origin Burma

Straight tail

Some tabby markings may appear

Large, alert ears with rounded tips

Slanted eyes

Short, glossy fur

Strong body

Fur on tummy is usually paler

Small paws — the pads are the same colour as the coat

CORNISH REX

Peculiar-looking, Cornish Rexes have soft, wavy fur. These cats love to play and need lots of attention to keep them entertained. They are naturally curious, clever and good-natured. Cornish Rexes need to be groomed at least once a week to keep their fur in good condition.

SMALL-MEDIUM

The first Cornish Rex, called Kallibunker, was born to normal parents. He had curly fur, but his littermates had straight fur.

FACT FILE

Eye colour Any

Fur colour Any colour and any markings

Character Playful and sociable

Special feature Wavy coat

Country of origin Britain

Small face with playful expression

Long nose

Slender, dainty body

Wavy, plush fur

Skinny tail

DEVON REX

The wavy fur of Devon Rexes is similar to the fur of Cornish Rexes. Their fur does not have the thick undercoat, so they often find warm places to sleep. They are big eaters, and need more food than other cats their size. Devon Rexes have wide faces with small noses, giving them a mischievous look. They love climbing and running.

SMALL-MEDIUM

While some Devon Rexes have even coats with plenty of loose curls, others have thin, short coats or patches that are almost bald.

FACT FILE

Eye colour Any

Fur colour Any

Character Sociable and energetic

Special feature Wags its tail when happy

Country of origin Britain

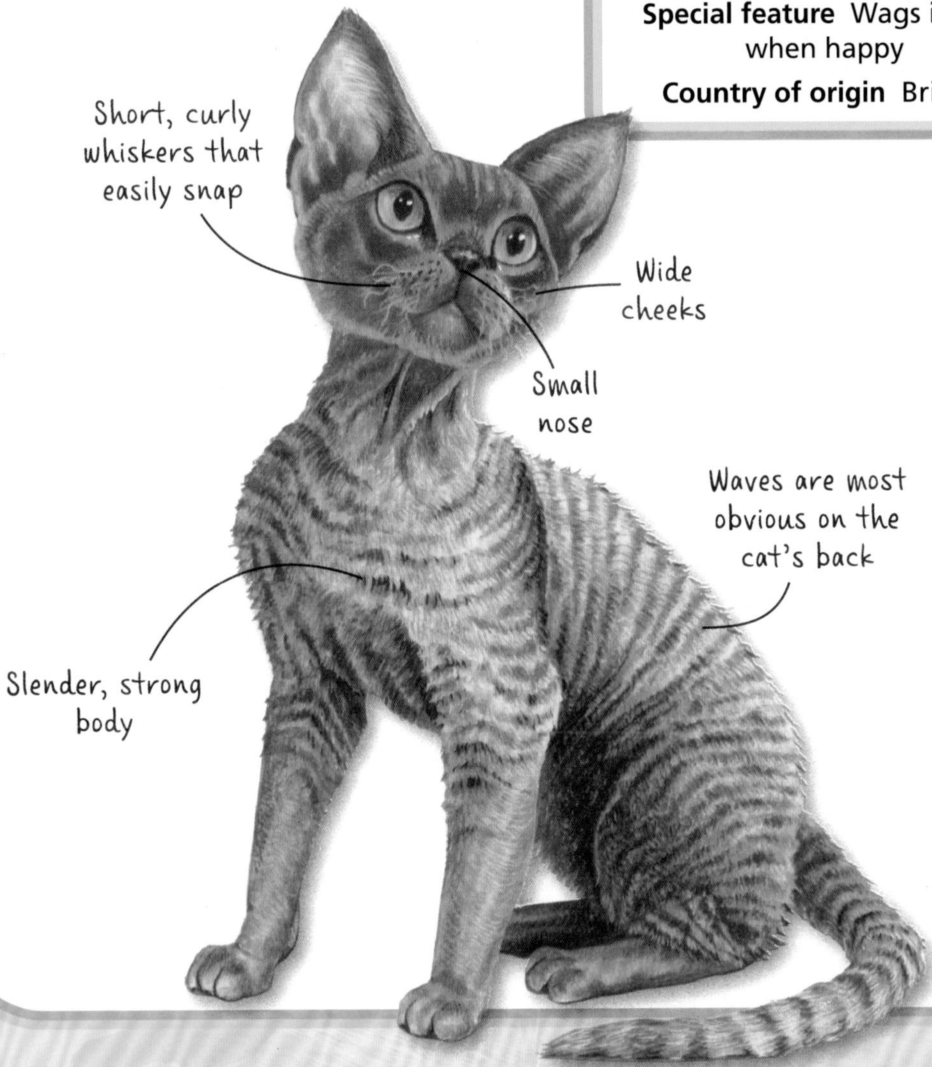

Short, curly whiskers that easily snap

Wide cheeks

Small nose

Waves are most obvious on the cat's back

Slender, strong body

EGYPTIAN MAU

Originally from Egypt, these cats are **thought to be related to cats honoured by the ancient Egyptians.** They are the only spotted breed of cats, although they also have many striped markings. Egyptian Maus are very active, and they love attention. They are one of the few cats that can be walked on a lead.

MEDIUM

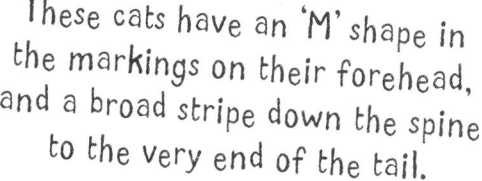

These cats have an 'M' shape in the markings on their forehead, and a broad stripe down the spine to the very end of the tail.

FACT FILE

Eye colour Light green
Fur colour Brown or black markings on silver, blue or black fur
Character Clever and busy
Special feature Can be walked on a lead
Countries of origin Egypt and USA

'M' marking
on forehead

Wide-set
ears

Dark stripe
down spine

Short nose

Almond-shaped
eyes

Dark flecks and
spotted markings

Elegant,
athletic body

HAVANA

Elegant Havanas look like Siamese, which they have been bred from. Attention-seeking cats, they like to be around people, and are especially affectionate. They often play with small objects, and may raise a paw and stare at their owners when they are being ignored. Havanas are graceful movers, with glossy coats and dainty, slender legs.

MEDIUM

Havana kittens may be born lilac or chocolate-brown in colour, with tabby markings that fade with time.

FACT FILE

Eye colour Green

Fur colour Deep brown

Character Sociable and intelligent

Special feature Long face

Countries of origin Britain and USA

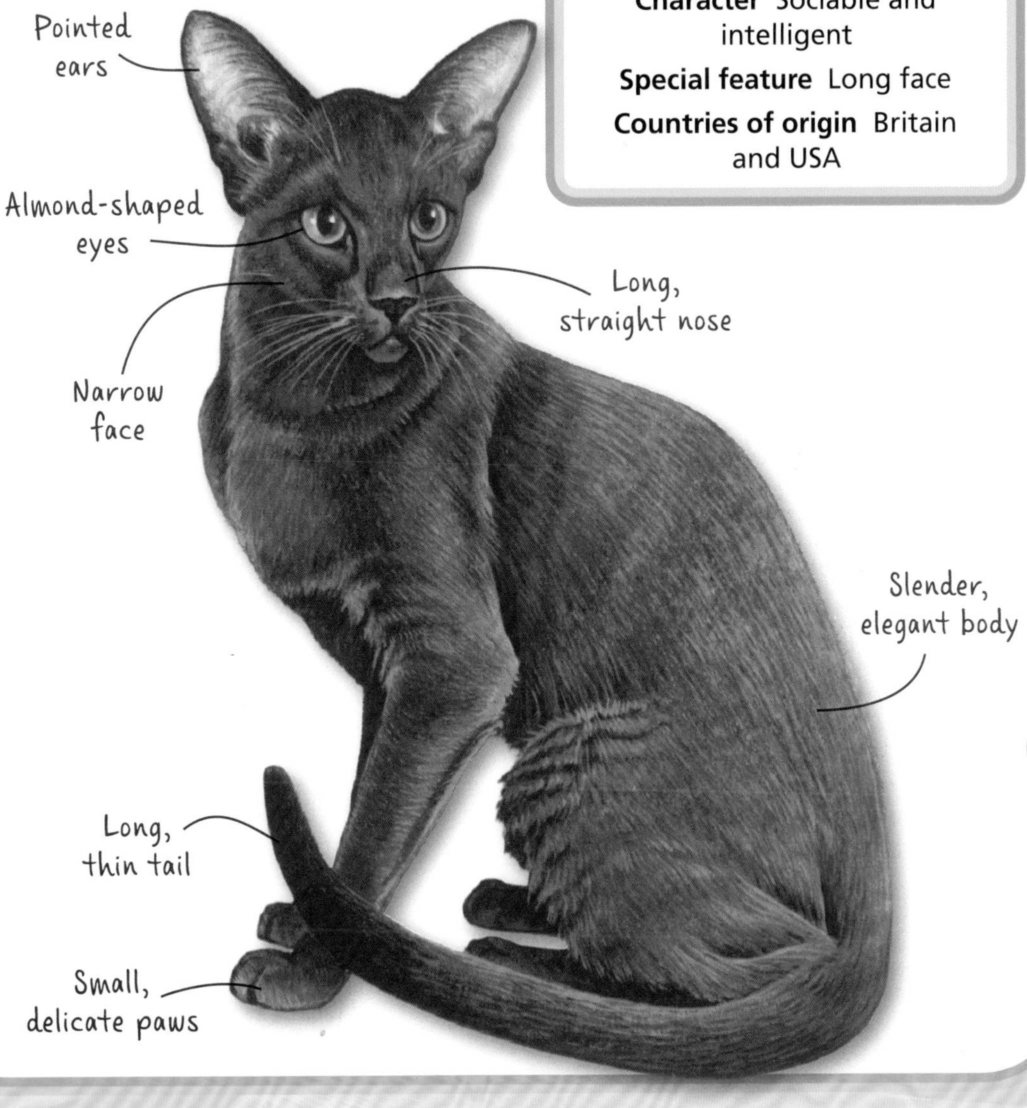

Pointed ears

Almond-shaped eyes

Narrow face

Long, straight nose

Slender, elegant body

Long, thin tail

Small, delicate paws

KORAT

One of the oldest breeds, Korats originally came from Thailand. They have a bright, alert expression and enjoy playing. Kittens sometimes have amber eyes, which turn green as they get older. Korats look similar to Russian Blues, but their eyes are paler green in colour. These cats have a thin coat, so they prefer to stay indoors during cold weather.

MEDIUM

The Korat was once believed to bring good luck to Siamese people.

FACT FILE

Eye colour Light green
Fur colour Blue-grey with silvery ends
Character Playful and sweet-natured
Special feature Eyes are an unusual shade of green
Country of origin Thailand

Large ears with rounded tips

Heart-shaped face with a wide forehead

Athletic, strong body

Rounded tip to tail

Dark-blue nose pad

Dark-blue paw pads

ORIENTAL SHORTHAIR

Shorthaired cats that are descended from Oriental cats are called Oriental Shorthairs. They include Havanas, Oriental Lilacs and Foreign Whites. The group also includes breeds that are not descended from eastern cats, but look like them. Oriental Shorthairs like a lot of attention and need company as well as plenty of toys. They are curious cats, and enjoy both exploring indoors and outdoors.

MEDIUM

These cats have unusually long noses, and wedge-shaped heads. They can be bred in more than 280 different colours.

FACT FILE

Eye colour Green or blue

Fur colour Various, including white, caramel, blue, tortoiseshell and black

Character Active and talkative

Special feature Long legs

Country of origin Various

Long, straight nose

Large ears

Long neck and head

Eyes are almond-shaped

Long, slender body

Long hind legs

Long, slender tail

RUSSIAN BLUE

Quiet cats, **Russian Blues are shy and elegant.** However, they are also playful and can even be taken outdoors on a lead. They like children and other animals as long as they can escape for some peace and quiet. Russian Blues can become very attached to their owners. Their fur is extremely dense and soft, and they like being groomed.

MEDIUM-LARGE

These friendly cats are also known as Archangels. They first came to Europe from a Russian port, called Archangel, as the travelling companions of sailors.

FACT FILE

Eye colour Bright green

Fur colour Blue

Character Home-loving and friendly

Special feature Can be walked on a lead

Country of origin Russia

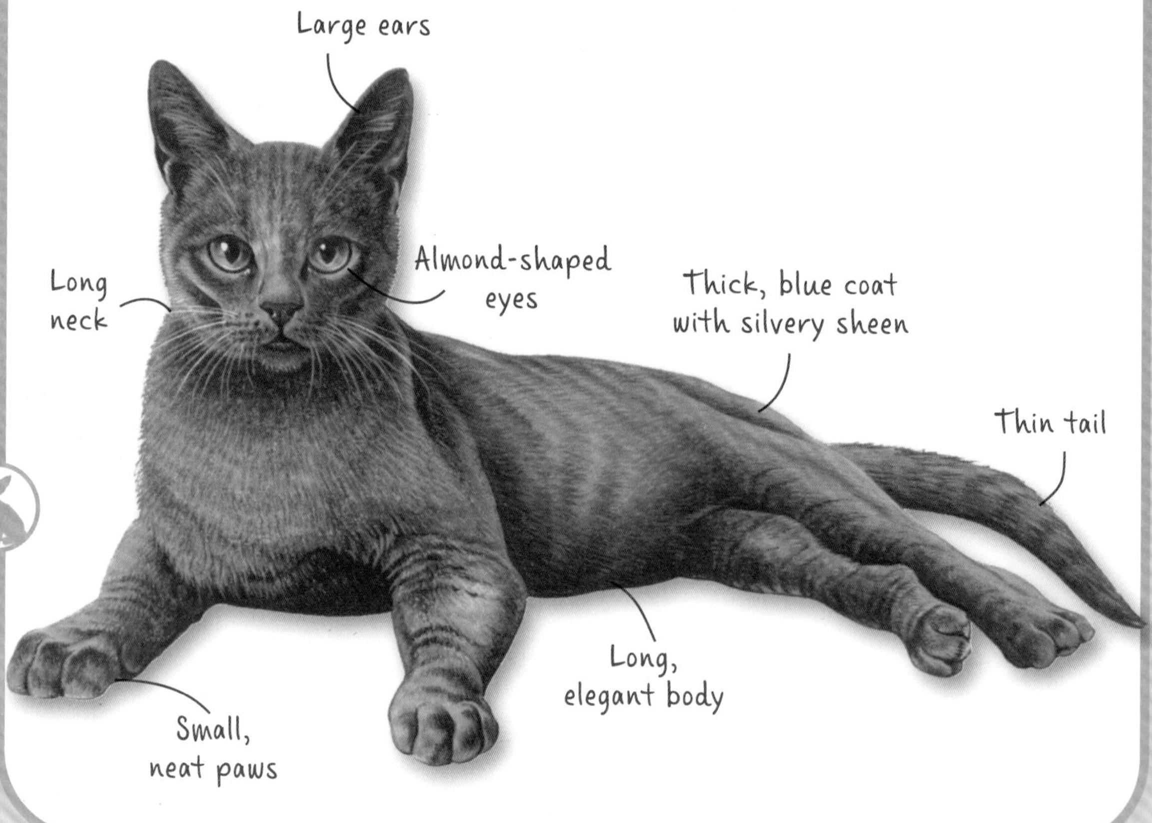

Large ears

Almond-shaped eyes

Long neck

Thick, blue coat with silvery sheen

Thin tail

Long, elegant body

Small, neat paws

SAVANNAH

These cats were originally bred by crossing Shorthairs with Servals, which are wild African cats. They were therefore named after African grasslands, called savannahs. It is a new breed, which has been developed since the 1980s. Savannahs can be a range of colours, and they are all playful, intelligent and sociable in nature.

LARGE

Savannahs can be walked on a lead, and can be trained to fetch things for their owners.

FACT FILE

Eye colour Yellow, gold, green or brown
Fur colour Brown, black or cream with tabby markings
Character Active and feisty
Special feature Likes playing with water
Country of origin USA

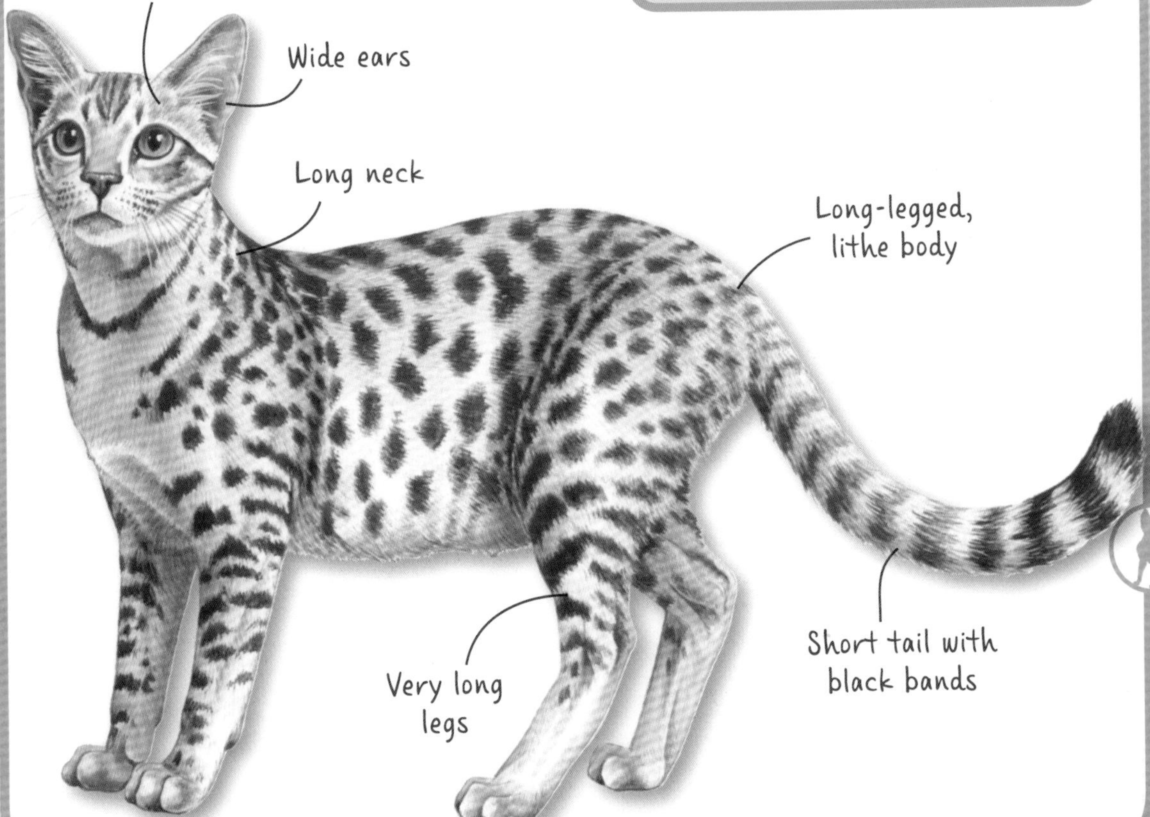

Broad face

Wide ears

Long neck

Long-legged, lithe body

Very long legs

Short tail with black bands

SIAMESE

Distinctive in both looks and personality, Siamese are demanding and reward their owners with great loyalty and affection. Siamese expect a lot of attention and are known to cry and yowl until they get it. They are clever and playful, as well as skilled hunters.

MEDIUM

Classic Siamese have 'points' — darker areas of fur on the face, ears, paws and tail.

FACT FILE

Eye colour Blue

Fur colour Shades of cream with darker points

Character Bold and clever

Special feature Cries rather than miaows

Country of origin Thailand

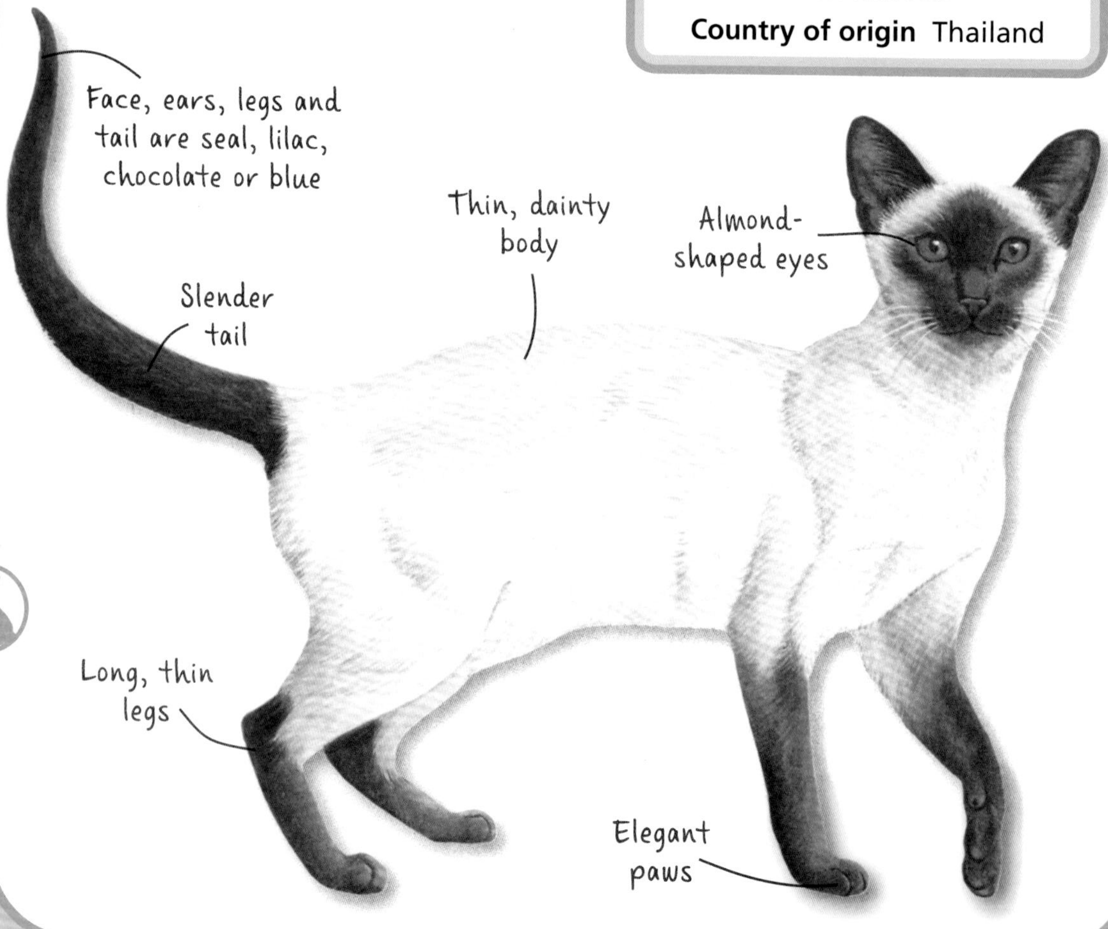

Face, ears, legs and tail are seal, lilac, chocolate or blue

Thin, dainty body

Almond-shaped eyes

Slender tail

Long, thin legs

Elegant paws

SINGAPURA

The dense but fine coat of the **Singapura is soft.** The fur is pale cream in colour on the stomach, chest and chin and flecked with darker, richer colours elsewhere. These cats have a particular liking for high places, and often sit at the top of posts or fences to watch what goes on below. They love attention and playing.

SMALL–MEDIUM

This is a rare breed that has been developed by breeding a Tabby from Singapore, in Southeast Asia, with blue Burmese cats.

FACT FILE

Eye colour Yellow, green or brown
Fur colour Dark gold to cream with darker flecks
Character Mischievous and friendly
Special feature Rare
Country of origin Unknown

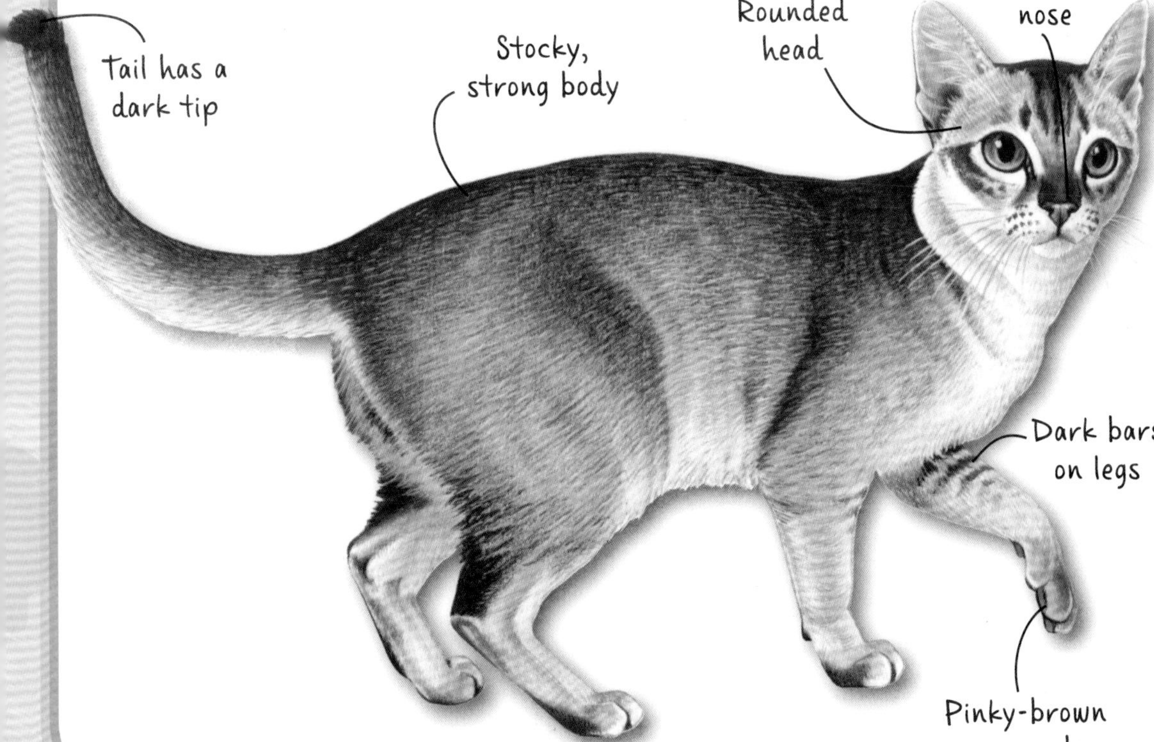

Tail has a dark tip

Stocky, strong body

Rounded head

Short nose

Dark bars on legs

Pinky-brown paw pads

SNOWSHOE

Named after their four white paws, **Snowshoes are bred from Siamese and American Shorthairs.** The kittens are white when they are born, but gradually darken and may have a range of markings. These cats need to be kept busy and enjoy company. Unusually, Snowshoes like water and have been known to go swimming.

MEDIUM

Snowshoes are white at birth, and their markings develop over the first three weeks. Like Siamese cats, their fur gets darker during cold seasons.

FACT FILE

Eye colour Blue

Fur colour Various but mostly blue, seal or chocolate

Character Playful and energetic

Special feature Likes being around water

Country of origin USA

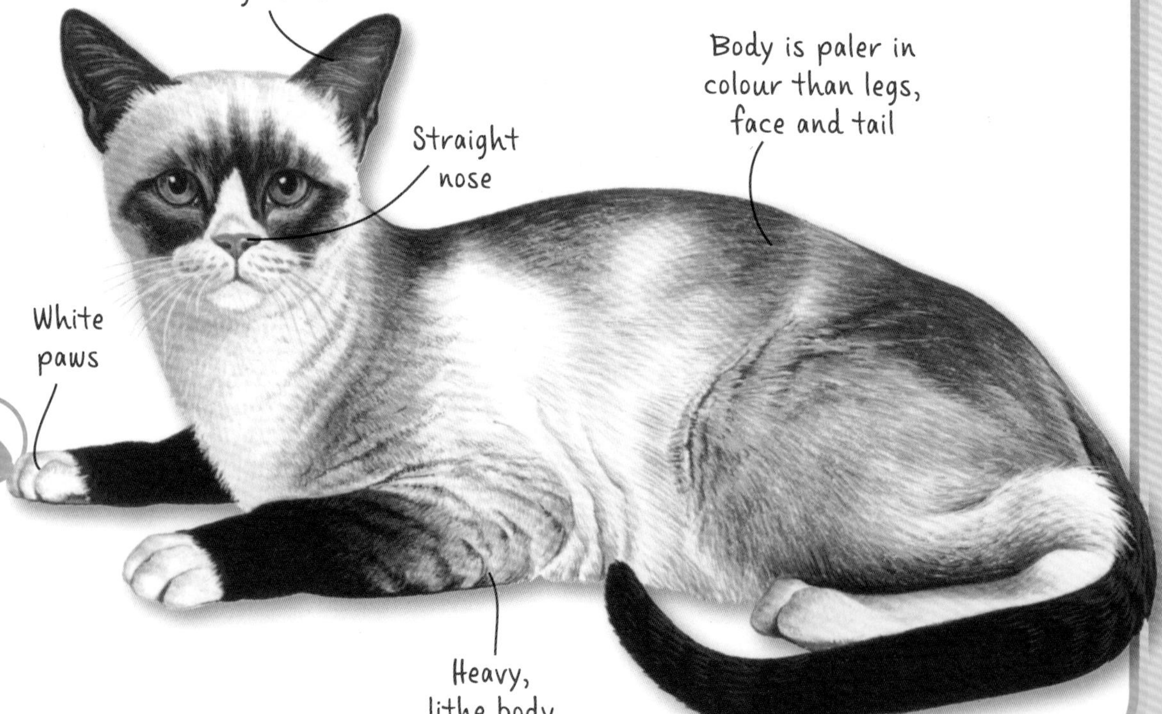

Large ears

Straight nose

Body is paler in colour than legs, face and tail

White paws

Heavy, lithe body

TABBY SHORTHAIR

A **popular breed, Tabby Shorthairs have existed for a long time.** Their coats come in two main patterns – classic and mackerel (which is more striped than the classic variety). Tabbies usually have strong characters and males, especially, can be quite independent.

MEDIUM-LARGE

The word 'tabby' comes from a place in the old city of Baghdad, called Attaibya, where striped silk was made and sold.

FACT FILE

Eye colour Gold, copper, green or hazel

Fur colour Cream to brown with dark markings

Character Independent and intelligent

Special feature Tabby markings

Country of origin Various

Short, wide tail

Strong, athletic body

Large, round eyes

Ears with rounded tips

Short, strong legs

Large, round paws

TABBY SPOTTED SHORTHAIR

Spotted Shorthairs are similar to other shorthaired Tabbies, but their dark markings are broken up into spots. They usually have a pale, silvery coat, which is dense and soft. Other colours such as blue and chocolate also exist. Spotted Shorthairs are strong, agile cats and they enjoy being outdoors, hunting and exploring. Their legs are quite short and well-muscled.

MEDIUM-LARGE

These cats are similar to an ancient Egyptian breed, which was honoured as a killer of snakes and evil serpents.

FACT FILE

Eye colour Yellow-green, green or hazel
Fur colour Silver-grey with dark markings
Character Gentle and good-natured
Special feature Spotted coat
Country of origin Various

Small, alert ears

Round eyes

Tabby markings appear as spots

Strong, athletic body

Soft coat

Short, strong legs

TONKINESE

Bred from Siamese or Burmese, Tonkinese are also known as 'Tonks' and 'Golden Siamese'. These good-natured cats are quite nosey, and like to be involved in anything that is happening. Tonkinese enjoy exploring outside, but they are happiest when around people. They use their voices a lot, and need plenty of toys and activity to keep them entertained.

MEDIUM

Tonkinese are known for their intelligence and unusually long memory. This means they can be trained, unlike most breeds.

FACT FILE

Eye colour Blue or blue-green

Fur colour Various, including cream, blue and dark brown, often with tabby markings

Character Friendly and curious

Special feature Loves running and jumping

Country of origin USA

Long, slender tail

Elegant, strong body

Large eyes set well apart

Soft, silky fur

Belly and chest are usually paler in colour

Oval paws

ANGORA LONGHAIR

These cats have soft, silky fur, without a dense, woolly undercoat. This makes them especially sleek and easy to care for. They were originally bred from Siamese, which gives them long, slender bodies. They love attention and 'talking' to their owners, and are playful, curious cats. The Angora Longhair is also known as the British Angora.

MEDIUM

When longhaired cats first came to Europe they were often described as 'angora', possibly after the Turkish city of Ankara.

FACT FILE

Eye colour Blue or green
Fur colour Various, from cream to black with various markings
Character Curious and chatty
Special feature Fine, silky coat
Country of origin Turkey

Wide, fluffy tail

Fur may be one solid colour, flecked or tipped with other colours, or with tabby markings

Ears are wide at base

Slanted eyes

Long, thin neck

Long, sleek body

BIRMAN

With bright-blue eyes, a pale coat and dark points, Birmans look like longhaired Siamese. The points can be lilac, chocolate, seal or blue, but their paws are always white. Their thick coats are not as dense as the coats of some other Longhairs, but they still need to be regularly brushed. These sweet cats have a loving, quiet character and a soft voice.

MEDIUM

According to legend, Birmans were once dark but became cream in colour after being touched by a golden goddess.

FACT FILE

Eye colour Blue

Fur colour Cream or beige with darker points

Character Gentle and loving

Special feature White feet

Country of origin Burma

Round, wide head

Silky fur

Long, heavy body

Dark points, except for paws

Fluffy tail

White paws

CYMRIC

These cats are easily recognized because they don't have a tail. Cymrics are bred from Manxes, although it is hard to breed truly tail-less Cymrics. Depending on the length of their tails, these cats are called Risers, Stumpies, Stubbies or Longies. Cymrics have a good nature, and love to jump up to high places. They are also known as Longhaired Manxes.

MEDIUM

Cymrics grow slowly, and reach adulthood when they are about 5 years old. They are also unusually heavy.

FACT FILE

Eye colour Any

Fur colour Any colour or pattern

Character Fun-loving and clever

Special feature Tail-less

Country of origin Isle of Man

Medium-sized ears

Broad, round head

Heavy, muscular body

No tail

Large paws

MAINE COON

An old breed from the USA, Maine Coons have developed thick coats to cope with cold weather. Their coats can be of many colours and patterns, and tabby markings are common. Maine Coons are affectionate cats, but they love the outdoors and need plenty of space to explore, hunt and play. They are known for finding unusual places to curl up and sleep, and often sleep outside.

LARGE

Maine Coons have furry tails that are at least as long as the body. They use their tail like a blanket to keep warm while sleeping.

FACT FILE

Eye colour Blue, copper, gold or green
Fur colour Various colours and markings
Character Friendly and playful
Special feature Loves the outdoors
Country of origin USA

Large ears with pointed tips

Large, long body

Long back

Silky top coat and dense undercoat

Large, strong legs

Fluffy tail tip

PERSIAN BLUE LONGHAIR

Like all Persians, Blues need plenty of attention. They need to be groomed regularly, so their fur doesn't matt or give them furballs. Kittens are usually born with some tabby markings, but this banding gradually fades to a solid blue coat. Persian Blues prefer to be indoors, and like to be fussed over.

MEDIUM

Queen Victoria had a special fondness for Persian Blues and even became the Patron of the Blue Persian Society.

FACT FILE

Eye colour Copper or orange
Fur colour Blue
Character Friendly and calm
Special feature Orange eyes
Country of origin Persia

Small ears set well apart

Large, round head

Flat face

Snub nose

Solid, stout body

Thick, short tail

PERSIAN RED SELF LONGHAIR

Due to their deep-orange coat, Red Self Longhairs are nicknamed 'Oranges'. However, perfect examples are rare, as they are often born with markings on their face, legs and tail. Red Self Longhairs are known for their round heads, snub noses and round ears. Sometimes they can be born with ultra-snub noses, which can cause breathing and skin problems.

MEDIUM

These cats were bred from Persians and Tabbies. Some Red Selfs are a solid colour, but it is normal for tabby markings to appear on their legs.

FACT FILE

Eye colour Copper or orange
Fur colour Deep orange
Character Sociable and affectionate
Special feature Snub nose
Country of origin Persia

Small, rounded ears

Snub nose

Solid, thick-set body

Short, fluffy tail

PERSIAN SMOKE LONGHAIR

Smoke Longhairs, or Smokies, are a type of Persian cat. Their smokey-blue undercoat is extremely dense, and usually tipped with black or blue. Some Smokies are tipped with tortoiseshell colours (white, red and black), but these cats are always female. Like other Persians, Smoke Longhairs are easy-going and relaxed. They do not need a lot of exercise, although they can easily become fat.

MEDIUM

Black Smokies have dark fur that is grey or silver near the skin. As they walk, the pale colour shimmers through.

FACT FILE

Eye colour Copper or orange
Fur colour Smokey blue
Character Calm and relaxed
Special feature Shimmering coat
Country of origin Persia

Snub nose and flat face

Deep-orange, large, round eyes

Large, round head

Solid, heavy body

Very long fur

Short, wide legs

Very fluffy tail

PERSIAN TABBY LONGHAIR

With similar markings to their shorthaired cousins, Tabby Longhairs have dense, **long fur.** Their coats are silky and require plenty of grooming to keep them knot-free and glossy. Original colours included brown, red or silver, but the tabby markings can vary both in colour and pattern. Mackerel Tabby Longhairs are especially striped. These cats are home-loving animals that enjoy company.

MEDIUM

Brown Tabby Longhairs are one of the oldest varieties, but they are also the most rare. They have brown–black fur, and copper or orange eyes.

FACT FILE

Eye colour Various

Fur colour Various base colours with tabby markings

Character Gentle and friendly

Special feature Dense fur

Country of origin Persia

Small ears with rounded tips

Wide head

Short snub nose

Solid, well-built body

Short, thick legs

Large, round paws

PERSIAN TORTOISESHELL AND WHITE LONGHAIR

With splashes of colour and long, fluffy fur, these cats are easy to recognize. Tortoiseshell and White Longhairs are members of the Persian family, but with the characteristic red and black blotches of a Tortoiseshell. Like other Tortoiseshells, these cats are all female. They are popular pets because they are not only attractive to look at, but have a gentle, affectionate nature.

MEDIUM

Blue Tortoiseshell and White cats have delicate blue and cream patches instead of black and red ones.

FACT FILE

Eye colour Various
Fur colour Various base colours with tabby markings
Character Gentle and friendly
Special feature Dense fur
Country of origin Persia

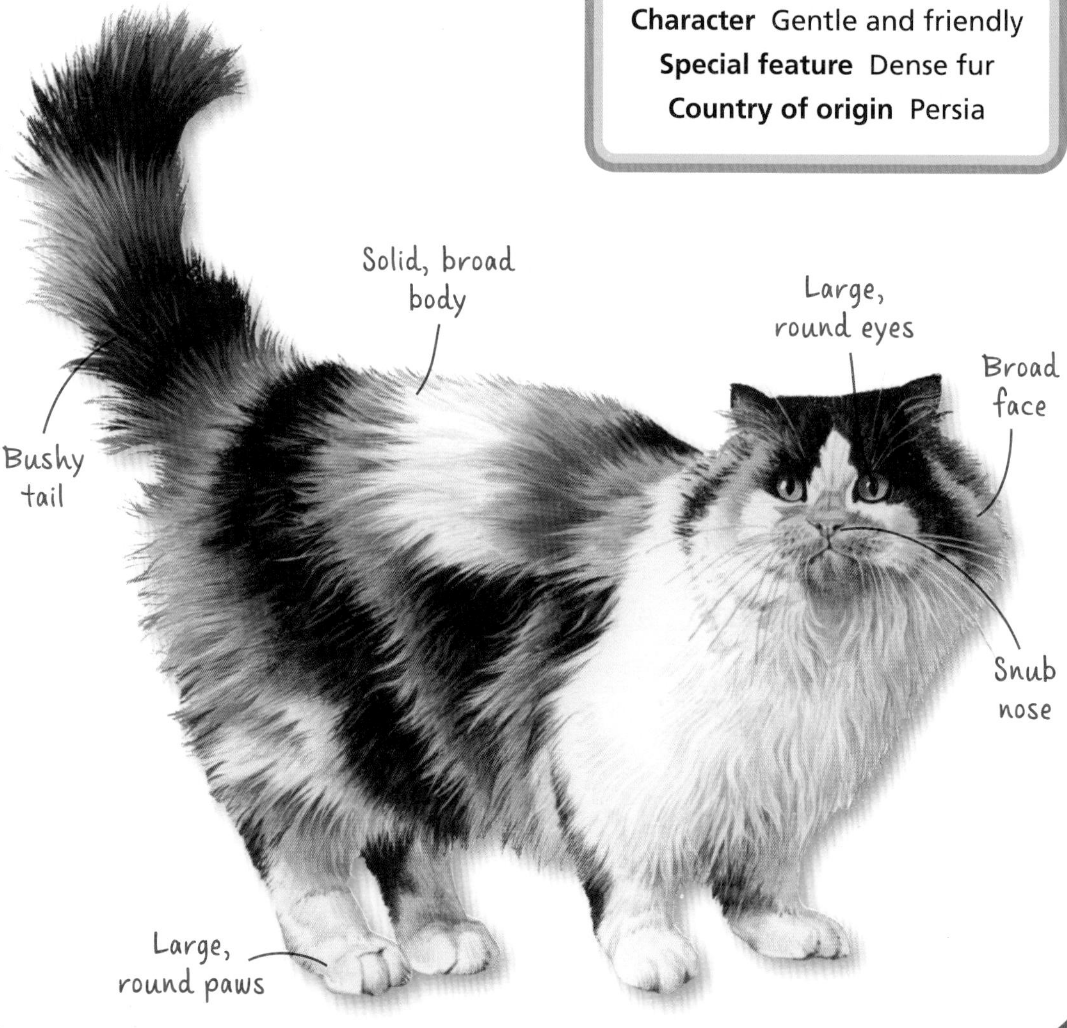

Solid, broad body

Large, round eyes

Broad face

Bushy tail

Snub nose

Large, round paws

PERSIAN WHITE LONGHAIR

Popular cats, Persian White Longhairs have bright eyes and dense, white fur. They are often bred for competitions, and were first developed by crossing Angoras with Persians. Persian Whites like to be groomed – by themselves or their owners. They should be brushed daily to prevent their fur from becoming knotted. These cats are friendly but not very active, and are happy to spend lots of time indoors.

MEDIUM

Most Persian Whites are bred with copper eyes, as blue is rare. However, some kittens are born with one blue eye and one copper eye.

FACT FILE

Eye colour Blue, copper or gold

Fur colour White

Character Placid and easy-going

Special feature Snow-white coat

Country of origin Persia

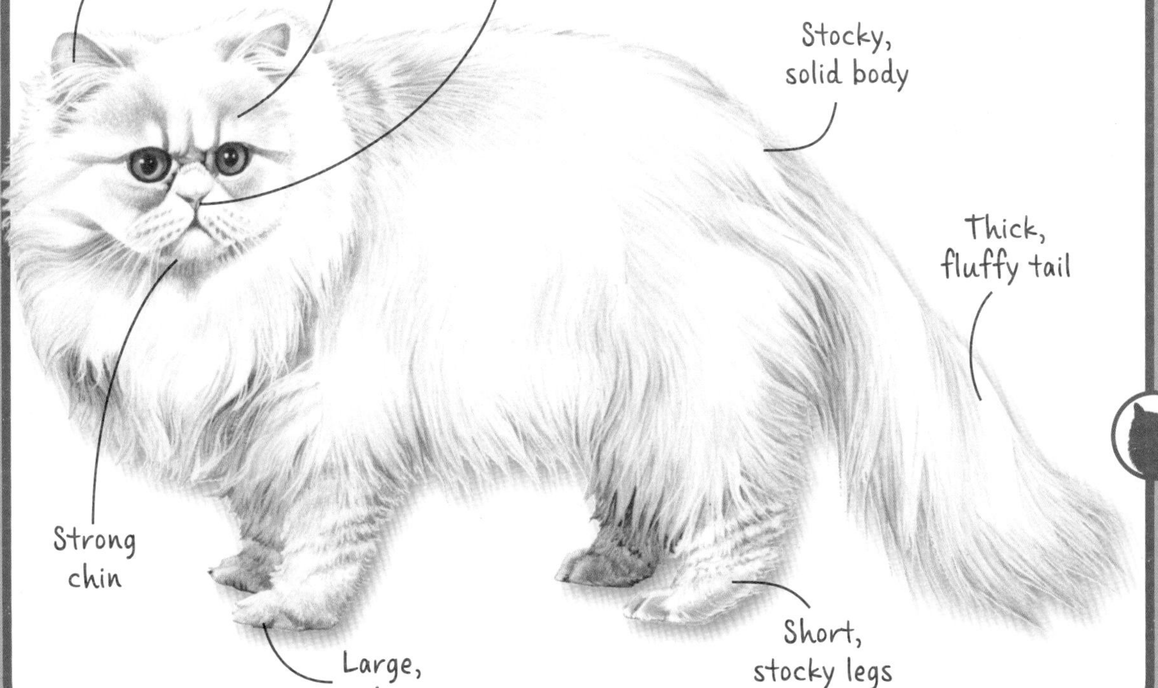

Small ears set well apart

Flat face

Snub nose

Stocky, solid body

Thick, fluffy tail

Strong chin

Large, round paws

Short, stocky legs

SOMALI

Fluffy Somali cats combine the elegance of Abyssinian cats with the long hair of Persians. The fur on their chest, tail and britches (backs of legs) is especially long. There are many coat colours, but each individual hair can have up to ten bands of different shades. Ruddy orange, apricot and warm copper Somalis are most common. These shy cats are active and like to explore, play and hunt outdoors.

MEDIUM

These clever cats are known to solve problems, such as opening doors and drawers, and even turning on taps.

FACT FILE

Eye colour Green, amber or hazel

Fur colour Various, including gold/brown, fawn and cream

Character Active and independent

Special feature Athletic

Country of origin USA

Large, pointed ears

Tufts of hair in ears

Elegant, long body

Shaggy fur

Long, thick, fluffy tail

TIFFANIE

These cats are Asian Longhairs that are descended from Burmese and Persian Chinchillas. Their hair is not as long as other Longhairs, although it still needs regular brushing to remain soft and silky. Tiffanies are extremely affectionate cats that follow their owners, calling for food or attention. They are known for their intelligence, and love to play with toys and people.

MEDIUM

Tiffanies first appeared in the 1980s and it is one of the newest breeds of cat. It takes many years to develop a strong, healthy breed.

FACT FILE

Eye colour Yellow, gold or green
Fur colour Various
Character Affectionate and clever
Special feature Coat is pale cream in kittens, and darker in adults
Country of origin Persia

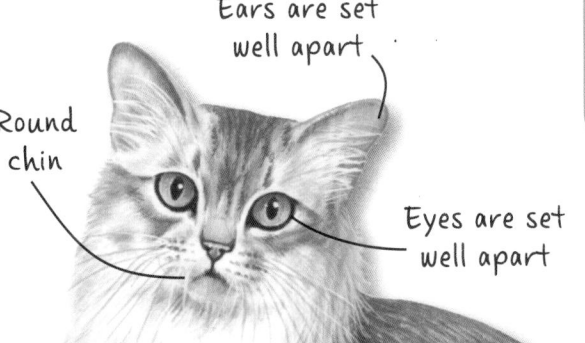

Ears are set well apart

Round chin

Eyes are set well apart

Elegant, muscular body

Slim legs

Long, fluffy tail

41

TURKISH VAN

These cats originally developed in an area around Lake Van, in Turkey. Unusually, they like water and are also known as 'Turkish swimming cats'. Their silky fur is long but without a thick undercoat, so it is glossy and soft, and does not knot as easily as other longhaired cats. They are active and intelligent cats that like to play.

LARGE

It is thought this is an ancient breed that survived in Turkish mountain areas for many hundreds of years.

FACT FILE

Eye colour Amber or blue
Fur colour White with some markings
Character Active and lively
Special feature Likes swimming
Country of origin Turkey

Large ears

Long, strong body

Markings on tail, head and base of ears

Broad chest

Delicate paws

Tufted tail

AMERICAN CURL

These unusual-looking cats are descended from a single female, called Shulasmith. Her ears curled backwards. Kittens start life with normal ears, which curl over time. American Curls are good-natured cats. They are known for enjoying games, even as they get older. They are loving and relish lots of attention.

MEDIUM

These kittens' ears curl and uncurl over the first 4 months of life, before becoming set into a permanent curl.

FACT FILE

Eye colour All colours
Fur colour All colours and patterns
Character Loyal and friendly
Special feature Curled ears
Country of origin USA

Ears are fully curled after 4 to 5 months

Slender, well-proportioned body

Silky coat

Fluffy tail

BALINESE

When Balinese cats walk, they sweep their long, fluffy tails from side to side. This breed is a longhaired Siamese. Although the fur is long, it is not dense, which gives the cat a dainty appearance and a fine, silky coat. Balinese have inherited some of the Siamese personality, and can be quite demanding although not always as talkative.

MEDIUM

Balinese cats developed when two normal Siamese parents produced longhaired kittens. These random events are called mutations.

FACT FILE

Eye colour Blue

Fur colour Shades of cream with darker points

Character Playful and good-natured

Special feature Demanding

Country of origin USA

Almond-shaped eyes

Ears may be tufted

Long, elegant neck and body

Small paws

Long hind legs

Tufted tail

44

HIGHLAND LYNX

First developed in the USA, the **Highland Lynx is a new, rare breed.** It was created by breeding a wild Desert Lynx with a Chausie. Highland Lynxes are always busy, exploring and playing. They are very friendly, too, and are often said to have doglike personalities because they are loyal and can be taught tricks.

LARGE

Highland Lynxes and Desert Lynxes look similar, but a Desert Lynx has straight ears. If a Desert Lynx and a Highland Lynx mate, their kittens have straight ears.

FACT FILE

Eye colour Gold, green or blue
Fur colour Various colours with a range of tabby patterns
Character Active and energetic
Special feature Many have extra toes
Country of origin USA

Large head

Curled ears

Tabby markings

Short tail

Long fur

Paws often have an extra toe

Muscular, strong body

JAPANESE BOBTAIL

Both longhaired and shorthaired Japanese Bobtails exist. Their coats are silky and smooth, and they are normally tabby or patterned with white. A common colour is 3-colour Tortie and White, which is black, red and white tortoiseshell. They are named after their short, 'bobbed' tail. These cats are playful, friendly and clever, and have a habit of raising one paw.

SMALL-MEDIUM

Japanese Bobtails are an ancient breed that appears in Japanese documents and pictures dating back more than 1000 years.

FACT FILE

Eye colour Any
Fur colour Various, especially 3-colour
Character Sociable and talkative
Special feature Raises one paw
Country of origin USA

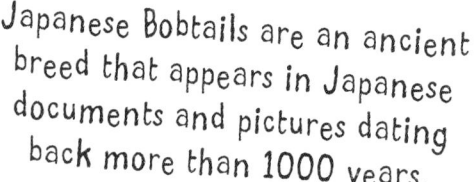

Eyes are slanted and sometimes of different colours

Lean body

Muscular, elegant body

Slender legs

Oval paws

Very short tail

LAPERM

LaPerms are descended from a kitten that was born bald, but then grew curly fur. Kittens born to LaPerm parents may be bald, have straight fur or curly fur. Some even have curly whiskers and ear-hair. LaPerms are clever and playful, and can form strong attachments to their owners. They love being cuddled and rub faces with people they like.

SMALL-MEDIUM

These cats are named after a 'perm' – a treatment that changes the structure of human hair to make it curl.

FACT FILE

Eye colour Any

Fur colour Any

Character Curious and demanding

Special feature Curly fur

Country of origin USA

Long, slender tail

Wavy fur

Almond-shaped eyes

Long neck

Strong, heavy body

Round paws

MANX

These Shorthairs are peculiar because they lack tails. They developed on the Isle of Man, an island off the coast of Britain. Some kittens are born with tail stumps, and Manxes are also known as Risers (tail-less), Stumpies, Stubbies or Longies. Manxes are energetic cats that enjoy climbing, chasing and playing with toys. Longhaired Manxes are called Cymrics.

MEDIUM

Manx cats are said to be doglike, and some of them will even fetch and bury their toys.

FACT FILE

Eye colour Various
Fur colour Various
Character Good-natured and friendly
Special feature Tail-less
Country of origin Isle of Man

Stocky, strong body

Round, wide head

Wide ears with slightly rounded tips

No tail

Hind legs are longer than the forelegs

Large paws

NORWEGIAN FOREST

This is an old breed from Norway – a cold country where an extra-thick undercoat is essential for an outdoor cat. Norwegian Forests, or 'weegies' as they are sometimes called, can cope with very cold weather and their fur dries quickly if it gets wet. They are clever cats that enjoy hunting and climbing, and will even investigate running water, looking for fish to catch. Their temperament is playful and loving.

LARGE

It is said that Vikings kept these cats as pets. They feature in many folk tales and are also known as 'fairy cats' in Norway.

FACT FILE

Eye colour Any

Fur colour All colours and patterns

Character Tough and adventurous

Special feature Quick-drying fur

Country of origin Norway

Long hair in ears

Large, oval eyes

Fur around legs, neck and chest is long and fluffy

Triangular-shaped face

Woolly undercoat is covered by longer top coat

Fluffy tail

OCICAT

Ocicats look like the wild cats, Ocelots; hence their name. However, they are not bred from wild cats, but from Siamese, Abyssinians and American Shorthairs. They have the beautiful markings of wild cats, but have a sweet, tame nature. They are energetic, adore company and can become bossy towards other cats. Ocicats can live for 18 years or more.

MEDIUM-LARGE

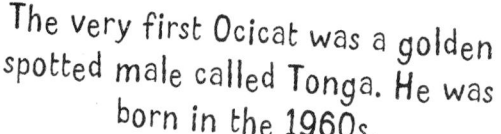

The very first Ocicat was a golden spotted male called Tonga. He was born in the 1960s.

FACT FILE

Eye colour All

Fur colour Various, with spots, tabby markings and dark tips to some hairs

Character Sociable and lively

Special feature Long-lived

Country of origin USA

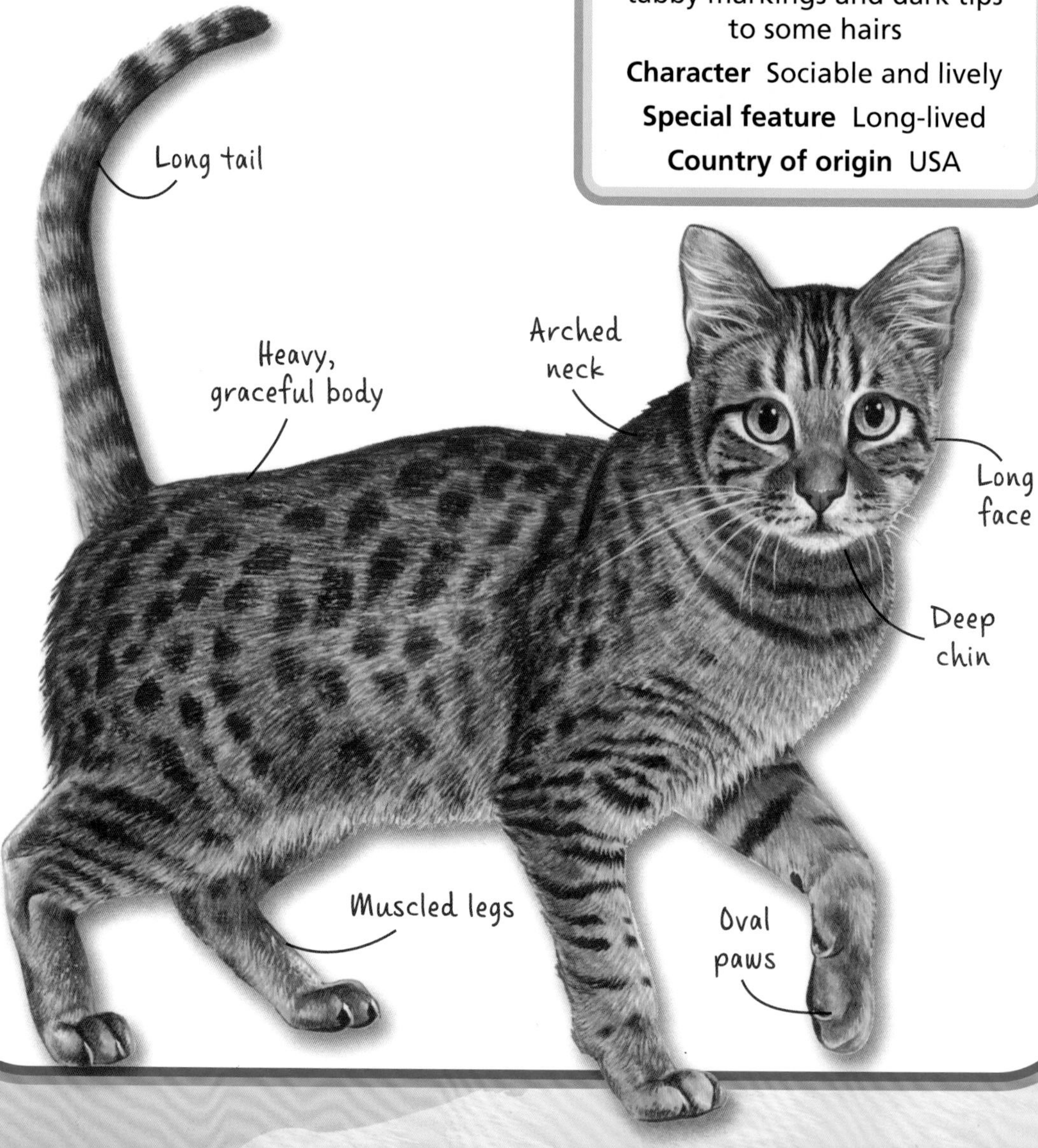

Long tail

Heavy, graceful body

Arched neck

Long face

Deep chin

Muscled legs

Oval paws

50

PETERBALD

These bald cats were developed in the 1990s, by breeding Don Sphinxes with Oriental Shorthairs. They can be described as nude, velour or brush, depending on how much fur they have. Nude cats are completely bald. These cats love attention and enjoy cuddling. Without a thick coat to keep them warm and protected, Peterbalds need special care and can even suffer from sunburn. They are also known as Russian Hairless cats.

SMALL-MEDIUM

Some Peterbalds are born with hair, but lose it. Hair loss begins on the head and continues down to the tip of the tail.

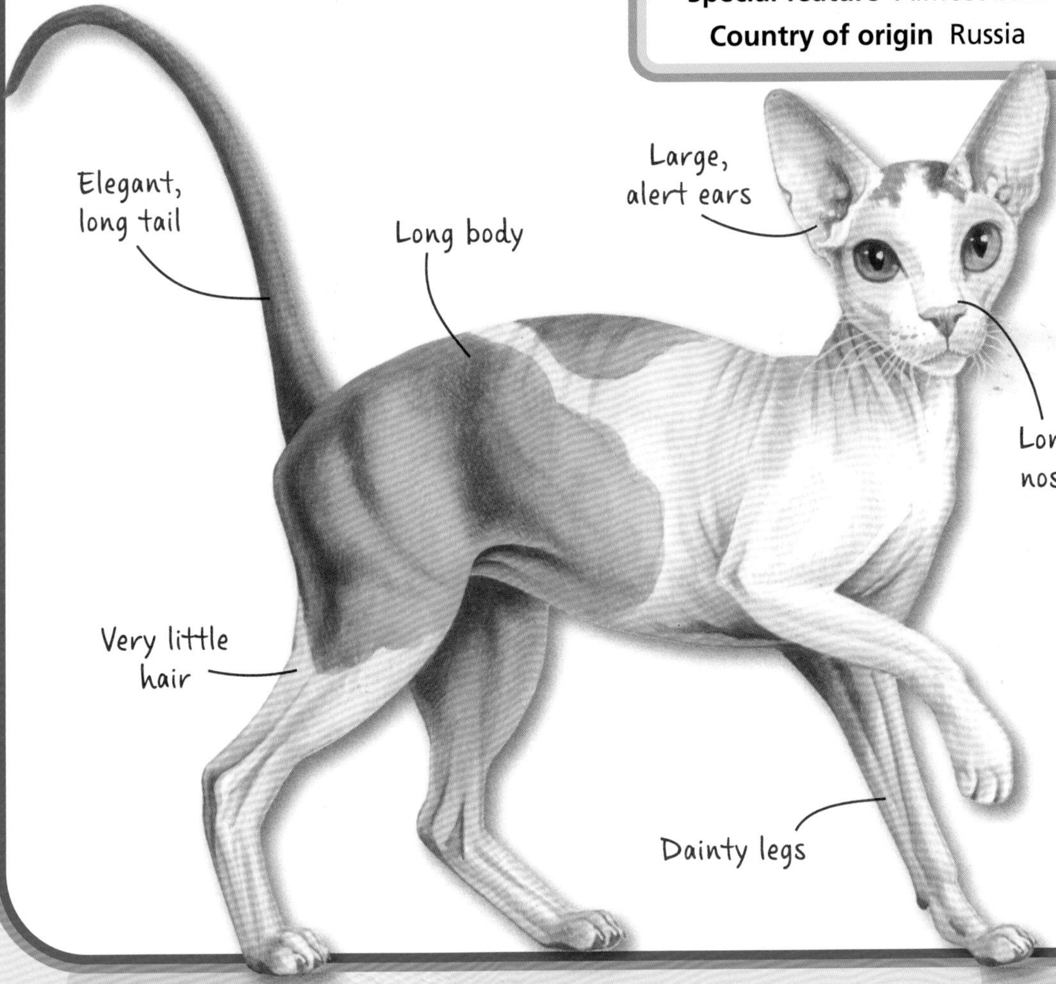

FACT FILE

Eye colour Greeny-gold or blue

Fur colour None

Character Sweet-natured and loving

Special feature Almost bald

Country of origin Russia

Elegant, long tail

Long body

Large, alert ears

Long nose

Very little hair

Dainty legs

PIXIE-BOB

A new breed, the Pixie-Bob has only been around since the 1980s. Although they resemble wild Bobcats, Pixie-Bobs are actually descended from domestic cats with spots and short tails. It takes these cats about 3 years to reach adulthood, whereas most cats mature in just one year. They rarely miaow, but like to chat with other cats and their owners by purring and chirping.

LARGE

Most cats have five toes on their front paws and four on their hind paws. Pixie-Bobs often have more — up to seven toes is normal.

FACT FILE

Eye colour Gold or gold with hazel flecks

Fur colour Shades of brown with markings

Character Loyal and bold

Special feature Short tail

Country of origin USA

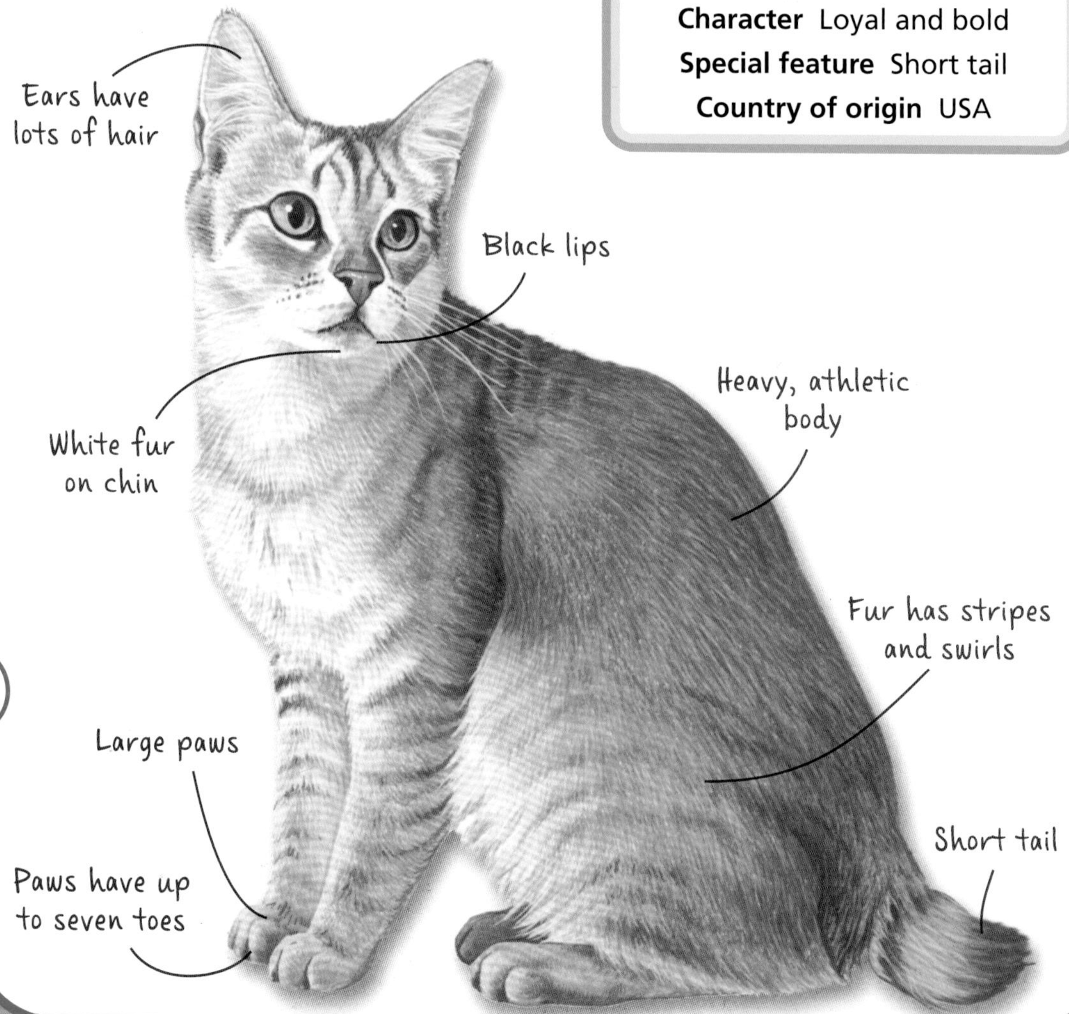

Ears have lots of hair

Black lips

White fur on chin

Heavy, athletic body

Large paws

Fur has stripes and swirls

Paws have up to seven toes

Short tail

RAGDOLL

It is thought that Ragdolls are descended from a mixture of Birman and Persian Longhairs. They are unique cats because, when picked up, they relax their bodies and become floppy, just like a ragdoll. Their coats are usually pale, with darker points on the face, ears and paws. Some Ragdolls have white patches, too. They have sweet personalities and enjoy receiving lots of attention.

LARGE

Ragdolls are large cats and, like other large cats, it can take them up to 4 years to reach adulthood.

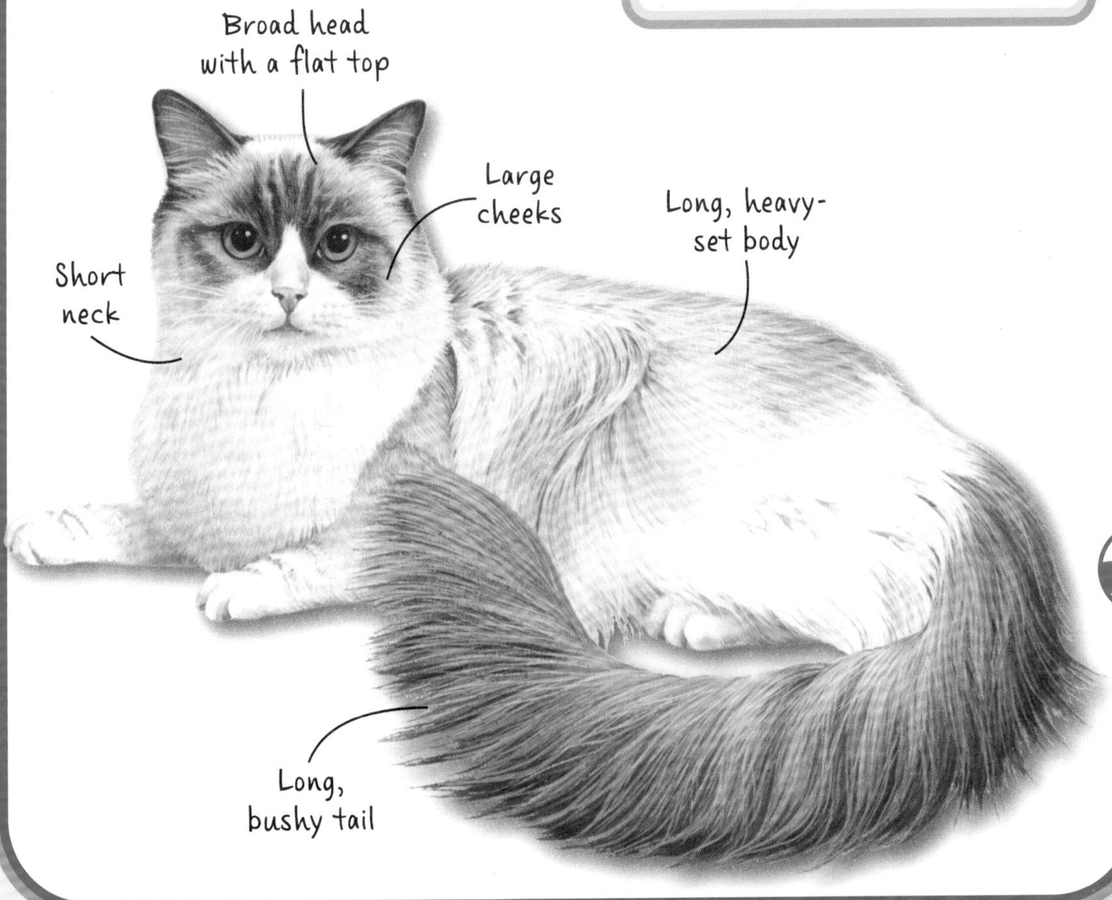

FACT FILE

Eye colour Blue

Fur colour Various colours with patterns

Character Trusting and affectionate

Special feature Floppy body

Country of origin USA

Broad head with a flat top

Large cheeks

Long, heavy-set body

Short neck

Long, bushy tail

SCOTTISH FOLD

These cats are named after their unusual ears, which are small and folded over. They cannot be bred together because the kittens will have back, leg and tail problems. They are laid-back, contented cats and especially good with children and other animals. Despite having strange ears, Scottish Folds are able to hear normally.

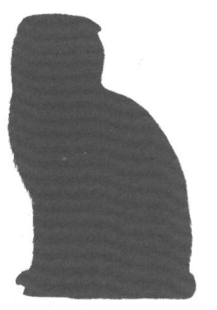

MEDIUM-LARGE

Kittens are born with normal ears, but after a few weeks about half of them will develop the characteristic folds.

FACT FILE

Eye colour Any
Fur colour Any
Character Friendly and gentle
Special feature Folded ears
Country of origin Scotland

Small ears are folded forwards

Broad face

Body is usually large

Short, round body

Large paws

SPHYNX

Although Sphynxes are famous for being bald, they usually have a fine layer of soft fur, or down. Their skin is warm and soft, and they do not sweat when they get hot. Sphynxes benefit from being washed regularly, and they should be in the shade to prevent sunburn. In winter, they mostly stay indoors to keep warm. They are cuddly and affectionate.

MEDIUM

The first Sphynx to be born was named 'Prune' because of her wrinkled, bald skin.

FACT FILE

Eye colour Any
Fur colour Any
Character Bright and friendly
Special feature Lack a proper coat of fur
Country of origin Canada

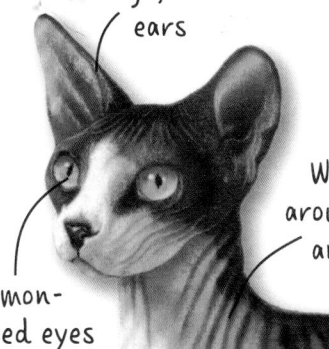

Large, alert ears

Wrinkles around neck and legs

Layer of fine fur all over the body

Lemon-shaped eyes

Slender, dainty body

Neat paws with long toes

GLOSSARY

Blue A deep-grey shade of fur that appears almost blue.

Breed All the cats that share a very similar appearance and personality.

Breeder A person who keeps animals to breed them, often to show in competitions or to sell.

Dense Fur that is formed when many strands of hair grow from a small area of skin. Dense fur is especially warm.

Domestic A cat that lives as a pet, rather than living wild.

Flecked A strand of hair that has more than one colour on it.

Groom To brush or clean an animal's fur.

Lilac A grey shade of fur with a pink tinge.

Mackerel A fur pattern that has prominent stripes.

Marbling A fur pattern that has streaks of a different colour.

Muzzle The nose and mouth of an animal.

Pedigree An animal that is a fine example of its breed. Pedigrees may be entered into competitions, and used to breed similar kittens.

Points The muzzle, paws, ear tips and tail tip of a cat may be darker in colour than the rest of its fur, and are called its 'points'.

Purr The raspy sound a cat makes in its throat when it is contented.

Red The colour of fur that is actually more like a pale orange than a red. Red markings often appear on a cream base.

Seal A colour of fur that is very dark brown – almost black.

Tipped Strands of hair that have dark tips.

Tortoiseshell Fur that is made up of hair with two different colours that appear in an irregular way all over the body. The result is a mottled brown that is also described as 'tortie'.

Undercoat A layer of dense fur that grows close to a cat's body and keeps it warm.